I am Christian

Cath Senker

Photography by Jenny Matthews

W
FRANKLIN WATTS
LONDON·SYDNEY

© 2005 Franklin Watts

First published in 2005
by Franklin Watts
338 Euston Road
London NW1 3BH

Franklin Watts Australia
Level 17/207 Kent Street
Sydney, NSW 2000

Acknowledgements
The author and publishers would like to thank the following for all their help
in the production of this book: David, Rosie, Jack, William and Felix Robarts;
the staff and children at St Thomas More RC School, Saffron Walden; Father
John of English Martyrs Church, Thaxted and his congregation.

The photograph on page 27 was kindly provided by
the Robarts family.

Photographer Jenny Matthews
Designer Steve Prosser
Series editor Adrian Cole
Art Director Jonathan Hair
Consultant Martin Ganeri O.P.

ISBN 978 0 7496 5929 5

A CIP catalogue record for this book is available from the British Library.

Franklin Watts is a division of Hachette Children's Books,
an Hachette Livre UK company.
www.hachettelivre.co.uk

Contents

All about me

My name is William and I'm eight years old. I live in a village in Essex. I've got lots of pets - two dogs, five chickens, a rabbit and a partridge!

My favourite lesson at school is English, and I love football. I play in the local boys' team at the weekend.

I live in the countryside and I think it's important to care for animals.

My family

I live with my Daddy, sister and brothers.
Rosie is 13, Jack is 11 and Felix is 2.

Daddy works
for a marketing
company.
Mummy died
when I was six.

Jack loves football like I do, and Rosie
enjoys drama. Our family is Catholic.
Rosie, Jack and I go to Catholic schools.

'We all help Daddy to prepare meals and to clear up afterwards.' Rosie

My Christian beliefs

Christians believe that God made the world. Jesus is the Son of God, and we follow his teachings. I believe that Mummy is with God and Jesus. They all keep watch over me.

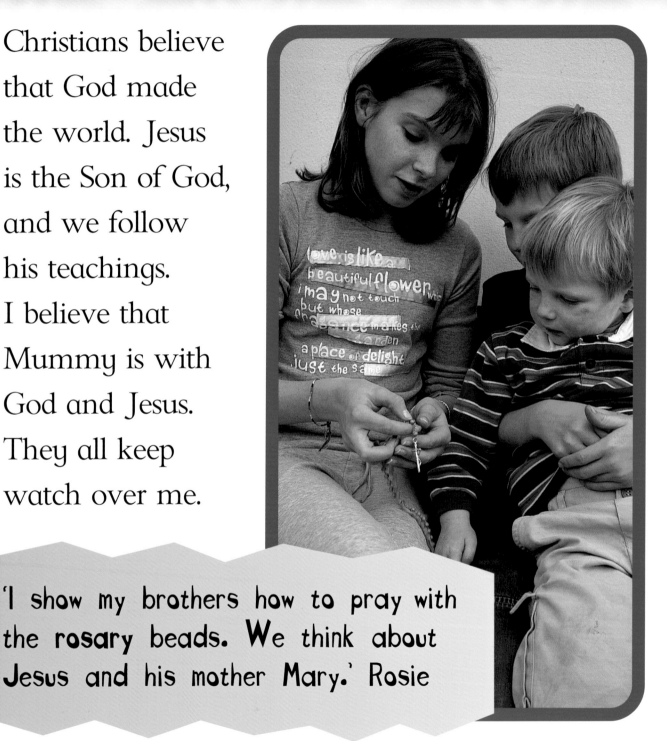

'I show my brothers how to pray with the **rosary beads.** We think about Jesus and his mother Mary.' Rosie

There are holy people called **saints**. We learn about them so we can try to follow their good example.

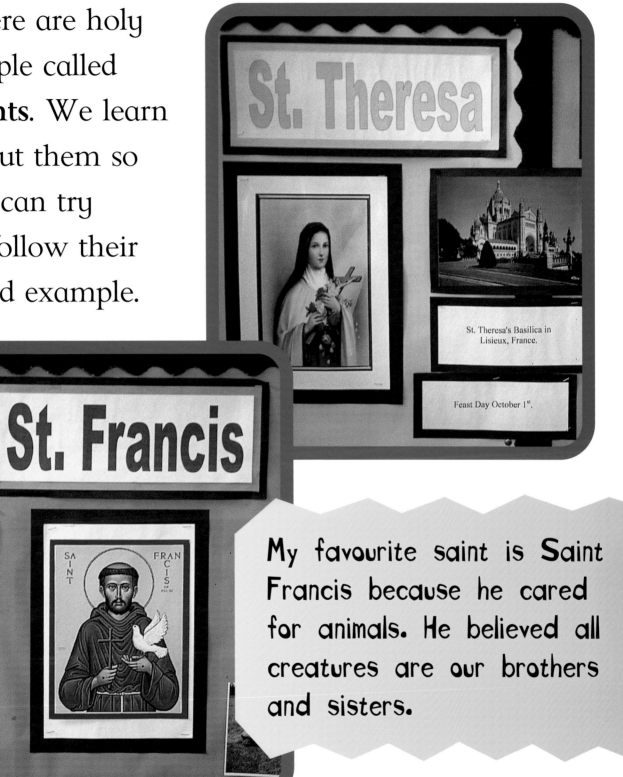

St. Theresa

St. Theresa's Basilica in Lisieux, France.

Feast Day October 1st.

St. Francis

My favourite saint is **Saint Francis** because he cared for animals. He believed all creatures are our brothers and sisters.

Our food

Usually, we eat what we like. During **Lent**, we give up a favourite food to remind us that Jesus spent 40 days in the desert without eating. This year I gave up chocolate, and Rosie gave up sweets.

At Easter, we hunt for chocolate eggs in the garden.

In autumn, we celebrate **harvest** festival. We bring fruit and vegetables to church and they're given out to elderly people.

At harvest festival, we thank God for making the crops grow.

Sunday

Sunday is a holy day for Christians.
We rest, pray and spend time together.
In the morning we go to church.

It's important to have a day that's different from the rest of the week.

Afterwards, we have Sunday lunch, often with friends from church. While we eat, Daddy explains the meaning of the priest's **sermon**.

'We have a family meal every Sunday so we can spend time together as a family.' William's Dad

Our church

We go to **mass** in the church. Our **priest** preaches a sermon. He often talks about how we should help needy people.

Rosie and I take the bread and wine up to the **altar.**

We pray and sing hymns - I prefer the modern hymns. Then we take **Holy Communion**. We remember how Jesus shared bread and wine with his followers just before he was killed.

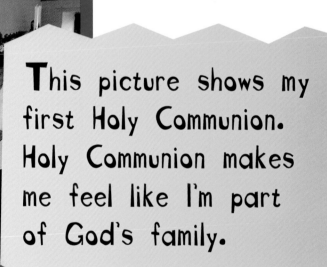

This picture shows my first Holy Communion. Holy Communion makes me feel like I'm part of God's family.

Our priest

Our priest is called Father John. He leads services in church. Sometimes, he visits our school to read us Bible stories and teach us new prayers.

Father John wears special clothes called vestments for mass.

Father John also helps to care
for people in the community.
He works hard to raise money
for the church and for charity.

'I know everyone in our Catholic
community. I do my best to help people
if they have a problem.' Father John

The Bible

The Bible is our holy book. The first part, the Old Testament, tells how God made the world. The New Testament tells the story of Jesus and the first Christians.

My favourite story is Jesus walking on water. When one of his followers, called Peter, put his trust in Jesus, he could walk on water too.

'The story shows us that, if we trust Jesus, he will help us through difficult times.' William's Dad

Saying prayers

We say prayers to tell God how good he is and to thank him for the world. We also pray to say sorry for doing bad things. Sometimes we ask God to help us, or other people.

At the start of prayers, we make the **sign of the cross**.

Before meals, we say a prayer
called grace to thank God for the food.
I sometimes pray at bedtime, too.

We can write our own prayers
for the prayer corner at school.

Learning about being Christian

At school, we have a Christian assembly every day. We also learn about Christianity and other religions in our R.E. lessons.

24

At home, Rosie often reads me Bible stories at bedtime. We each have a crucifix above our bed.

Jesus died on the cross, so the crucifix reminds us of him.

In the hall at home there is a prayer table for Mummy, with a candle and photos.

I pray to God to make things better and I pray for Mummy in heaven.

Christmas

My favourite festival is Christmas, when we celebrate Jesus's birthday. On Christmas Eve, we stay up late to go to **Midnight Mass.**

'We set up our Nativity scene with models of Mary, Joseph, Jesus and the animals, ready for Christmas.' Jack

On Christmas Day, we sing carols in church and then go home for Christmas lunch. We pull crackers and open our presents. That's the most exciting bit!

Glossary

altar The holy table at the front of the church where the priest stands.

crucifix A model of a cross with a figure of Jesus Christ on it.

harvest The time of year when the crops are gathered in.

Holy Communion A church ceremony in which people eat a small piece of bread and drink some wine to remember the last meal that Jesus ate with his followers.

Lent The season of 40 days before Easter when Christians think about things they have done wrong.

Nativity scene A model of Jesus and his family in the stable where Jesus was born.

mass A Catholic church service at which people take Holy Communion.

Midnight Mass A service held at midnight on Christmas Eve to celebrate Jesus's birth.

priest The person who leads religious ceremonies and carries out religious duties in the Christian Church.

rosary A set of beads that Catholic people use for counting prayers as they say them.

saints People that Christians see as holy because they lived particularly good lives.

sermon A talk about a religious topic.

sign of the cross Making a cross sign on your body by touching your forehead, chest, left and then right shoulder.

Websites

RE:Quest - Introduction to Christianity
www.request.org.uk/main/basics/basics.htm
About God, Jesus, the Bible, becoming a Christian, forgiveness and other topics.

Christianity for children
http://atschool.eduweb.co.uk/carolrb/christianity/
All about Jesus' life and teaching, Christian beliefs, celebrations and festivals, symbols, the Bible, worship and different groups of Christians.

I go to a Catholic church
www.request.org.uk/main/churches/catholic/catholic01.htm
A child describes what happens at a Catholic church.

The RE site for Infants: Christianity
http://infants.theresite.org.uk/index.html
Has information about the Church, Bible, festivals, God, symbols and following Jesus.

The BBC RE site for Juniors: Christianity
www.bbc.co.uk/religion/religions/christianity/features/whatitmeans
Five people talk about what it means to be Christian, plus information about holy days, customs and worship.

Note to parents and teachers
Every effort has been made by the Publishers to ensure that these websites are suitable for children; that they are of the highest educational value, and that they contain no inappropriate or offensive material. However, because of the nature of the Internet, it is impossible to guarantee that the contents of these sites will not be altered. We strongly advise that Internet access is supervised by a responsible adult.

Index